To the
Tanskis

MW00943015

ALI-
MAMA
A FERAL CAT'S TALE

by

NANCY KARAS MARKOFF

Enjoy the read!

Nancy Markoff

Ali-Mama: A Feral Cat's Tale
by
Nancy Karas Markoff

ISBN-13: 978-1492813620
ISBN-10: 1492813621

First Printing

Cover Design by Danielle Correia
Cat Illustration © clipart.com/Getty Images

ALI-MAMA

A FERAL CAT'S TALE

A FERAL CAT'S TALE

In 1999, a feral cat came into my life who, by her very definition, had no name. This would soon change. Diligence, tenacity, passion and love allowed me to befriend this complex, glorious creature. I was able to witness first hand a feral cat's life, and how she raised her kittens. This is a very unique story, one which most people have never had the opportunity to experience. Do I have your attention? Good, then let me take you through my journey of A Feral Cat's Tale.

Wikipedia defines the term feral cat as "a cat that is a descendant of a domesticated cat that has returned to the wild. It is distinguished from a stray cat, which is a pet cat that has been lost or abandoned, while feral cats are born in the wild; the offspring of a stray cat can be considered feral if born in the wild."

My definition of a feral cat is a frightened feline looking for someone to love.

ALI-MAMA

We were living in a gated community in south Florida when my husband, Allan, first saw a gray and beige tortoiseshell cat with the most mesmerizing green eyes walking past our house. It was quickly obvious to us that she was feral, as the moment we opened the door she flew in the opposite direction. My husband is a crazed animal lover and has this insatiable "need to feed" (a characteristic I battle with to this day). He immediately wanted to feed her, I did not. I stuck to my guns for about an hour. Then out came the gefilte fish and the rest, as they say, is history.

I am sure you already see the writing on the wall. Yes, my husband insisted on feeding her on a regular basis. At first she would just eat and run. Imagine our surprise when one day we saw her sunning herself on our back patio. It seemed that she was inviting us to come out for a tête à tête but we were quite mistaken. She kept her distance and lounged guardedly by the pool. Eventually, she stopped fleeing for her life when I walked out the sliding glass door.

During this adventure I read everything about a feral cat that I could get my hands on. In most cases a feral cat's life is relatively short, usually no more than two years, due to disease as well as a great number of predators. Their entire day is spent searching for sustenance. They have to depend on their hunting prowess, not a Fancy Feast can. Their primal instinct tells them if they cannot find food they will perish and so will their offspring.

The "as of yet nameless feral cat" had a sharp sense of survival which never ceased to amaze me. Her flight response was finely honed and trust was not an option for her. The more aloof she was the more I was determined to win her over. Sounds easy—right?

Wrong. It took another year before I was able to even get close to her. But I was determined, and by then she was appearing on a daily basis to sample mealtime at the Markoff's.

By this time she was more comfortable with us and did not head for the hills every time we ventured outside. I decided to use food to befriend this beautiful creature who had us in the pads of her paw, even though she still would not let us pet her. For some reason, I knew instinctively when she was about to appear and so to the refrigerator I went.

First, I would sit on the patio far enough away so as not to spook her. Slowly, very slowly, I would approach by crawling towards her. Then I would throw her a piece of cheese. Eventually, she began to come towards me to take the food. As time went on she became friendlier but remained always guarded, ready to flee.

A FERAL CAT'S TALE

We began leaving the sliding glass door open and she started to venture inside, one paw at a time. She soon realized I was always an easy touch for a snack. When she heard the refrigerator door open and the sound of the plastic wrap on the cheese she became quite brave and ventured further into the house. She got quite comfortable being in the living room with us and would occasionally rub up against my leg. I would position myself so I could quickly pick her up from behind and put her on the couch with me.

That turned out to be a big mistake! Unbeknownst to me her name should have been "fleabag." We soon had the most disgusting infestation of fleas. We had to fog the house and put flea repellent on her neck. Not so easy with a feral cat. Thank goodness by this time she was a tad more secure and would allow some limited physical contact. In no time at all we were flea free and I made it a point to apply repellent on a monthly basis.

The cat became a frequent visitor and when she was MIA, I would call her in a high pitched tone, "Here kitty, kitty" (original don't you think?). She always seemed to come running from wherever she was. During this time we were traveling back and forth between New York and Florida. When we were in New York our next door neighbor in Florida, Bea, was the surrogate meal provider. Even though Kitty had been on her own for a long time, I always worried about her when we were gone. The moment we came back I would call "kitty, kitty" and she would come flying.

After one of our trips, Bea informed me she had renamed Kitty to Ali. When I looked at Kitty, I had to agree she should have a more important name than Kitty. I had called her mama many times, so Ali-Mama it was.

One day, when Allan and I were sitting by the pool, we heard squeaking in the foliage behind us. Upon further inspection we discovered kittens hidden about three feet off the ground in the fronds of a palm tree.

We were so excited. We had to exercise great patience not to get too close to the kittens. The next day we tiptoed out to the palm tree only to find they had been "abducted." I later learned that after giving birth, the mother cat or "queen" waits about three weeks and then relocates them. We were so disappointed.

Ali-Mama would still visit on a regular basis. One evening shortly after our first discovery of the kittens, she came for dinner and lounged on the patio for some petting time. When she got up to leave Allan and I went into surveillance mode.

We covertly (or so we thought) followed her to see where she was stashing the kittens—but there was no way she was ready for us to find those babies. She kept walking in circles around the neighborhood until it became quite clear she was purposely taking us on a wild goose chase.

My husband was determined to find the kittens and he masterminded a scheme for us to use walkie-talkies so both of us could follow and see where she was going. Just imagine two grown, fairly sane-looking people, lurking around the neighborhood with walkie-talkies looking for a cat. In spite of our efforts, she still would never lead us to those kittens.

A week or so later, guess what showed up in our back yard? Three beautiful kittens. One was a tortoiseshell, another was beige and the third black. There is nothing cuter than a kitten and Allan and I spent our days just watching the shenanigans of these precious babies.

Most people do not get to see a feral cat raise its kittens, but Allan and I got to do just that. It was fascinating to observe Ali teaching her kittens how to hunt and kill.

When they were ready to stop nursing, she brought them a dead salamander (a Florida staple for felines). She put it in front of them and batted it around, as if to spur their interest in this new delicacy. The kittens played around with it but were not interested enough to consume it.

A few days later she brought another appetizer. This time the salamander was slightly alive and flopping around a bit. They started swiping at it with their paws but seemed to remain unaware that very shortly this would be their main source of nutrition. They would try to nurse but Ali-Mama was having none of it.

Every time they would approach their designated teat (from birth each kitten nurses from the same nipple and finds its way there by picking up its own scent) Ali would swat them out of the way. They soon learned Ali meant business and was no longer willing to be the local milk bar. Again, she presented them with a live salamander and they finally got the drill, realizing since they could no longer nurse they better try to ingest the next best thing—salamander a la king.

I also learned on this journey that when kittens reach 12 weeks of age, the mama, knowing she has prepared them for life as a feral cat, literally kicks them out of the nest—perhaps a lesson we humans should consider when raising our children. Sure enough, once the kittens were three months old Ali no longer wanted anything to do with them. The awareness of time was amazing—12 weeks on the dot was the turning point. Ali no longer wanted to interact with her kittens and she was rather bitchy about it. She would actually chase them away and when you were being chased by Ali you did not challenge her (a raccoon learned this lesson the hard way but I will save that for later in this tale).

When it was clear Ali had had enough of the mother thing, Bea would take the latest litter to our veterinarian who would spay and neuter them and put them up for adoption. We were always sad when the kittens had to go but we knew it was necessary to get them off of the feral cat treadmill. It was always in the back of my mind to capture Ali and get her spayed, but it was a task which was almost impossible. Although she trusted me, there was always the feral part of her that would not succumb to total bodily manipulation. I could go so far and then she would bolt.

During this time with Ali she became more

attached, especially to me, and the feeling was quite mutual. She always had the ability to tug at my heart strings. As a feral she developed a trust with me that was so special. Occasionally she would even venture upstairs and snuggle up on a shelf in our bookcase.

Time passed and we were in New York for most of the fall of 2000. We came down to Florida at the end of October and all I could think of was calling Ali and hoping she would hear me and come running. She did not disappoint. When I saw her I knew she was "with kitten." She grew larger as each day went by and now she even allowed me to massage her very large pregnant belly. I do not know who enjoyed it more.

With no need to hunt for food, since her lodging at the Markoff's included a meal plan, Ali spent most of her time on our back patio. We grew closer still and formed a bond that was never broken. She was a pregnant mama and acted the part, lazing every day by the pool and drinking the pool water. In the beginning of November she disappeared for a few days and when she reappeared it was clear she had given birth. Ali would still show up every day for a meal and hang around for a bit then go on her way. Allan and I went into surveillance mode again but we never were able to find the kittens. I knew that she would move them three weeks after giving birth so I hoped that she would bring the kittens to us as she had before.

The day before Thanksgiving I happened to catch her walking into our bedroom closet with something swinging from her mouth and I knew that she had brought her babies home to grandma and grandpa. A few minutes later she left and came back with another hanging fur ball and deposited it into Allan's shoe, next to the other kitten. I was so amazed that this creature knew that she could trust us with her kittens. According to my research the odds of ever truly befriending a feral cat and gaining their trust are next to nil. Unless kittens are handled by a human within six to eight weeks of birth they never learn to trust that human touch. Ali-Mama was the exception, as you have begun to see during this Feral Cat's Tale.

There were only two kittens this time. One was a female black and orange tortoiseshell and the other, a male, looked like a Russian Blue. They were so tiny they actually fell into Allan's shoes. We were amazed about how different they were from each other and could not believe they came from the same litter. This spurred my curiosity and sure enough, I learned that cats are induced ovulators which mean they release an egg only during copulation. Since they are in heat for about a week it is quite probable that a feral cat would have different mates during that time, which accounts for kittens in the same litter having different fathers.

We were so excited to have kittens in residence. We spent most of our time (we even gave up golf) just observing with delight Ali-Mama mother those babies.

It had been about three weeks since the kittens first took up residence in our closet and it wasn't long before they were up and about. We made sure we handled them as much as possible. We wanted them to get used to and come to enjoy our human touch. When we first picked them up they spit and struggled, but they warmed to our touch after a few seconds. We could not believe that Ali-Mama allowed us to handle her babies. The connection and love I felt for Ali kept growing. She truly trusted us.

ALI-MAMA

We saw them climb out of Allan's shoes and take their first steps. We also saw the female take her first poop. Kittens do not urinate or defecate the first days of their lives. The mama keeps them squeaky clean and licks and stimulates them to evacuate. One day while they were still in the closet we heard the female, who by the way was the first to do everything, make little peeping sounds. We then discovered it was her first poop. Extra! Extra! It was time for the little darlings to be ushered outside to the patio, pronto. They made the transition to their new residence without a hitch and settled in as if they had been there forever.

It was becoming quite obvious that these little rascals were going to become full-fledged members of our family, so off to the veterinarian we went for their first check-up. Upon our arrival we were asked what their names were. When I looked at the black and orange little girl Peanut Butter popped into my mind and when I looked at the blue kitten, a boy, I had the ingenious idea to call him Blue—original don't you think?

They weighed in at one ounce each. They got their shots and the vet was amazed and perplexed that neither one of them had worms or fleas. Almost all kittens are born with worms. More later on the worm thing but no worms for the Markoff cats. Yea! The flea debacle was more than enough parasite infestation for us.

At the beginning of December the kittens were about five weeks old and it was time for us to go back to New York. I had a very hard time leaving them even though we would only be gone for two weeks. They had become so much a part of our lives. Peanut would fall asleep on my chest and Blue was the follower, watching everything his sister would do. Talk about mischievous—they were so fun! They did nothing but play. They climbed the curtains and scooted underneath the treadmill (a favorite place to hide). They would shoot around the house at a hundred miles an hour, then fall asleep in an instant wherever they dropped.

Kittens do know how to have fun but the fun stopped when they tried to play and bite their mama's tail. Ali-Mama was a no-nonsense mama. When she whipped her tale around they would try to pounce on it and bite it. Very soon they learned that was not acceptable behavior. Mama was on a mission to teach her babies all they needed to know to survive in the wild as she had. Her kittens learned exactly how they were supposed to behave. That is another lesson we could learn as parents raising our children.

Allan's business is video surveillance. Because of my concerns about leaving Ali-Mama,

Peanut and Blue, he set up cameras outside on the patio so we could watch them from New York. I was worried because of the many predators in Florida, but the idea of being able to watch them on the cameras allayed my fears somewhat. Having watched Ali-Mama mother those babies, I knew that she would keep them safe. I set up the chaise lounge with a skirt of towels around the perimeter so they were shielded from the outside but could still go in and out at will.

When we got to New York, the first thing Allan would do in the morning was access the cameras and watch the outdoor gymnasts in action. The kittens ran and played with abandon but they were also conscientious students, learning to survive from Ali-Mama.

Bea would feed and nurture them in our absence. We always kept in touch by telephone and she would update us with the current gymnastics of the day. I could not get back to Florida fast enough.

We arrived back in Florida around the middle of December. The feline family was all intact and welcomed us with open paws. We snuggled and cuddled with them all, making up for all the time we were away.

One evening in the wee hours of the morning we heard a ruckus outside where the kitten family was sleeping. Allan jumped out of bed and looked outside. He saw Ali-Mama holding at bay the largest raccoon we had ever seen. She had placed herself between the striped predator and the kittens and there was no way she was going to allow that monster to get to those babies. Allan quickly ran and found a weapon (a tennis racket) to ward off the coon. He flew out the sliding glass door in pursuit of the masked imposter, but we learned that night that Ali needed no assistance.

A FERAL CAT'S TALE

She had chased the raccoon off in short order and came back to check on the babies. With all the commotion Peanut had wedged herself between the screen and the sliding glass door. She was spread-eagled and was hanging onto the screen like a cartoon character. Once we retrieved her we could do nothing but laugh.

Towards the end of December a cold snap arrived. Allan and I were very conflicted about whether or not to bring the kittens inside. We were in the process of discussing this when we noticed three felines sitting all in a row staring at us through the sliding glass door. I am sure they were hoping that we would cave and bring them in. The decision was made. I went to the pet store to purchase kitty litter and a litter box and proceeded with what I anticipated to be the daunting task of training this cat family toilet hygiene. Instead, as soon as I put Ali and the kittens in the litter box, they knew what to do.

Of course, once they were in the house they settled in like they owned the place. Strangely enough, Ali-Mama appeared to be quite content in her new role as house cat. She was still free to come and go but she spent most of the time lolling around in the sun and teaching her kittens the facts of life.

The Christmas holidays of 2000 came and went and it was time to go back to New York for a couple of weeks. As we had seen her do before, I knew that soon Ali-Mama would abandon these little darlings and probably chase them from her territory. Since Peanut and Blue were now members of our family we decided to take them back to New York with us. Armed with their health certificates and cat harnesses onto the plane the Markoff family went. Little did I know that

A FERAL CAT'S TALE

I should also have been armed with a tranquilizer—not for the cats but for me. Peanut meowed the entire flight while Blue cowered in the bag.

We stayed in New York for a couple of weeks and returned to Florida the third week in January. Peanut and Blue were at the 12-week mark and I was concerned how Ali-Mama would react upon seeing them. In my heart I thought maybe she would show a mother's love and embrace them with open paws. Wrong. She was agitated and especially took it out on Blue, the male. She went after him and it was clear we had to keep them apart. It was hard for me to see Ali who was such a loving, attentive mother become so aggressive and detached from her offspring. Sometimes nature is hard to understand. Peanut and Blue stayed inside and Ali stayed outside—a compromise that seemed to suit everyone.

Although Ali stayed outside now, I always

ALI-MAMA

Pre-natal massage appointment

spent time with her on the patio. She came to love the attention and seemed rather content to let the little monsters reside in the house. Allan and I spent most of our time just observing their behavior. Peanut and Blue remembered the treadmill game, but this time when they tried to run under the treadmill they got stuck. They had grown so fast they no longer were able to fit underneath. If cats have expressions we swear we

A FERAL CAT'S TALE

Ali-Mama on her journey to domesticity

saw a perplexed look on their faces as to why they once fit and then didn't.

They were growing by leaps and bounds and by the end of February it was again time to go back to NY. I dreaded the trip but we went meowing all the way.

Upon learning about the ethical issues surrounding feral cats my husband and I felt strongly that our kittens needed to be spayed and

ALI-MAMA

Ali a.k.a. Fleabag depositing a crop of fleas onto the couch

neutered. In our research we found out there is an overwhelming feral cat population in the United States, estimated to be about 60,000,000. You read that right—60,000,000, a number that is totally unmanageable. When unsterilized ferals are released into the cat population, the queens can give birth as early as five months old. Since gestation is approximately 65 days, they can have three or more litters each year. These feral cats

A FERAL CAT'S TALE

Markoff Spa - Lunch by the pool

are wild animals and their instinct is to produce as many offspring as possible to ensure survival of the species. I have read on the internet that a female can exponentially produce 350,000 offspring during her lifetime. This number is probably an urban legend and it seems that the more accurate number is around 100 to 400.

The Humane Society of the United States, realizing the need to stop the suffering

ALI-MAMA

Ali-Mama's milk bar - Nursing on the patio

and euthanization of this overpopulation has developed a program called Trap-Neuter-Return (TNR). Once trapped cats are sterilized, and vaccinated against rabies, they are eartipped. Eartipping is a humane, surgical removal of a quarter-inch tip of the left ear. This identifies the cat as having been sterilized, which prevents an already sterilized feline the stress of re-trapping and unnecessary surgery. Then they are returned

A FERAL CAT'S TALE

Ali and litter loitering

to areas benevolent to ferals. Over time, it is the hope that the overpopulation and subsequent suffering of these glorious creatures will be brought under control.

We had Peanut and Blue spayed and neutered at around five months of age and they settled into living permanently in New York without a hitch. Allan and I traveled back and forth to Florida on a regular basis and my mom became surrogate

ALI-MAMA

Another hard day at the Markoff's

grandma, stopping at our New York house daily to care for the cats and to offer some playtime.

As they grew we saw their personalities develop. Peanut the female was almost an exact replica of her mama. Where Ali was gray and beige, Peanut was black and orange. Peanut was always the first to explore the world. The most glaring similarity was Peanut's "catitude." It was virtually identical to Ali-Mama's.

A FERAL CAT'S TALE

There really is nothing cuter than a kitten

You could feel Peanut's intense sense of self-confidence. It was as if she believed she had control of her own destiny. What was even more evident was that she knew she had control over her pet humans. Most cats tend to be very aloof and for some reason humans just about jump through hoops to gain acceptance of their feline housemates. Because it is so difficult to attain you only need to have a cat show you a little love

Enjoying gefilte fish du jour

and attention to make you want to spend all your time recreating those moments. Cat people surely understand this all too well.

Blue, the male, who really looks blue, is a big mush. From my experience the males tend to be that way. He loves being held and looks for any opportunity for a love session with any human who has a lap. While he seems to lack the confidence that Peanut has, Blue has replaced

A FERAL CAT'S TALE

Baby Boo

it with a loving dependence on his humans. The female species of humans and felines are quite complex. The males are all about love. I think nothing more needs to be said.

During that summer we decided to sell our house in Florida and purchase another in the same community about two miles away. We moved into the new house around Thanksgiving. The old house was sold but we would not close

ALI-MAMA

You are interrupting Peanut's bath time

until after the season in February. It was a wonderful opportunity to have my mother-in-law and her husband come to Florida and stay in Ali-Mama's house (anyone who has a cat knows that it is their house, not yours) for the winter season. It gave me more time to decide what to do about Ali-Mama. I was quite torn because this was her territory and I could not imagine moving her to our new home. On the other hand, I could not

A FERAL CAT'S TALE

Peanut and Blue's snuggle time

imagine life without Ali-Mama. At least I had a few months to figure it out.

When they say the apple does not fall far from the tree they are so right. Allan got his love for animals from his mom. While we were in our new house his mom nurtured and cared for Ali-Mama at our old one. Ali was rather stand-offish with her but certainly allowed her to be the food bank. I would go back to

ALI-MAMA

Boy, were we lucky Mama-Ali found the Markoff's

visit and call "here, kitty, kitty" and she always came running.

When Allan's parents were ready to go back to New York, Ali-Mama graced us with another litter in the bushes by the pool. I decided that I had to try to move her to our new house. The kittens proved to be the best decoy.

Once our old house was vacant, my daughter Michelle and I went to a pet store and purchased

A FERAL CAT'S TALE

Time for a cheese break

a large crate. We put the crate in the bedroom closet, then went out to the patio, picked up the three kittens and placed them in the crate. Ali-Mama looked at me as if to say, "What the hell?" She followed me into the closet and saw the kittens in the crate. She cautiously proceeded into the crate but spooked by the noise of the door closing, she bolted. I thought maybe we would have to abandon our plan but I placed a can of

ALI-MAMA

Peanut's nap time with Nancy-Mama

tuna in with the kittens and waited. That did the trick. Ali went in and I was able to close the door and off to our new residence we went.

My daughter and I had some concert on the two mile drive from old house to new. Ali-Mama yowled the entire way and we were very glad when we pulled into the driveway and were able to de-car. I had already prepared a cozy niche for the new arrivals. I put the beach towel that was always

A FERAL CAT'S TALE

Ali-Mama and Michelle -
Doesn't look like a feral cat to me!

used for Ali and her kittens underneath a shelf in the office closet. Michelle and I carried the crate to the office and lovingly placed her kittens in the little kitty niche.

The office had a sliding glass door that opened onto a large courtyard which was perfect for the new family. They would be well protected but still able to be part of Florida outdoor living.

Ali-Mama clearly was glad to be let out of

ALI-MAMA

Ali-Mama assisting with work...

prison and bolted out the sliding glass door into the courtyard. She stayed outside quite a while exploring her new digs and then came back to check on the babies. For the most part Ali seemed to be unfazed by the entire adventure, which was amazing. I can only guess that she trusted me to do no harm to her or her kittens.

They all adjusted quickly and before long the kitten's eyes were open. Now that they were

A FERAL CAT'S TALE

...then she needed a nap

ready to start exploring their world, I decided it was time to transition them to the outside. The courtyard allowed us to observe them from just about every room in the house and I must say it again—there is nothing cuter than a kitten.

One kitten was blue-gray with white boots (Missy), one was a light brown tabby (Lulu) and one was all blue (Baby Boo). They all had the most beautiful green eyes, just like their mama.

ALI-MAMA

Did someone call my name?

Because they were so little when we picked them up to place in the crate they never went through the little spitting tantrum their older siblings had. They were instantly lovable and had the most wonderful personalities. They all soon discovered what Ali had known for quite a while, the Markoff spa was the place to be. They had a deluxe pool front room with access to the courtyard, three squares a day and unlimited massages.

A FERAL CAT'S TALE

Ali-Mama laying in the sun on the towel
that cradled all of her kittens

Missy was the one with the hereditary catitude. She was a loner and always looking to cause some trouble. One day she went missing. After about an hour I saw a strange kitten come into the family room. She looked like Missy minus the white boots. I thought perhaps a stray had gotten into the house. Upon closer observation, I realized it was Missy. She had gotten into the fireplace and the white boots

ALI-MAMA

Blue - The Lion King

were really gray ash. I had little ash paw prints all over the house.

Baby Boo was my husband's favorite and she adored him. One day she was in Allan's lap while he was watching a football game. When his team scored my husband put his arms up and screamed "touchdown!" My husband has a very distinctive, loud voice and really gets into this football thing. When he looked down at Boo, she was three

A FERAL CAT'S TALE

Tai on moving day

times the size with all her fur standing on end. Although she was frightened, she never left his lap.

Boo also figured out in short order what the refrigerator was all about and anytime my husband opened the door, Boo was there to share Allan's snack. She also decided to abide by modern day health advice which states that breakfast is the most important meal of the day. Every time my husband sat at the kitchen table for his cereal, Baby Boo was sitting upright on the table right next to the bowl so she could share with him "the most important meal of the day." I trust anyone who is not a cat person will not be reading this because the thought of a cat on a table would really send them over the edge—perhaps a good thing! Cat people will understand.

The previous owner of our new home had drapes that puddled onto the floor with loads of fabric. Shortly after we moved in, Missy was again nowhere to be found. Not wanting to repeat the ash paw prints all over my floor, I headed to the fireplace. She did not repeat that escapade, so we searched until we finally gave up. Three hours later, as I walked through the living room, out walked Missy from underneath the puddle of satin. She'd been there all along and appeared very well rested. She took a long stretch and had an expression on her face as if to say, "Was anyone looking for me?" Cat people also understand that cats have expressions.

We were fast approaching the time when Ali-Mama would be ready to boot the kittens out of the nest. I had to go back to New York so the responsibility of getting the kittens to the veterinarian landed on Allan's shoulders. I can tell you it was a job he was not looking forward to. He had grown very close to Baby Boo, who always gazed at him with goo-goo eyes. If we could have figured out a way to keep them as ours we would have, but it was not in the cards so off to the vet they went. It was a very sad car ride for Allan but he made sure that they would have great homes and actually bribed the girls in the vet's office with a bonus if the kittens were placed quickly. (They also had no worms—vet still perplexed.)

Ali-Mama appeared quite content and did

not seem to miss her offspring. Allan came back to New York a week after the kittens were gone. He was very glad to see his New York babies and Blue, the male, stuck to him like glue. Allan and I had many serious discussions about the importance of capturing Ali and getting her spayed. We knew it was crucial to finally take this feline out of the feral cat colony and to stop her from contributing to this very serious overpopulation problem. She was very sly and seemed to intuitively know whenever I was thinking about capturing her. We agreed that the next time we were in Florida it would be our priority.

We flew down at the end of the summer committed to the task of having Ali spayed. I arrived at the house and opened up the sliding door and called "kitty, kitty." Ali came flying over the eight foot courtyard wall very, very prego. She was very glad to see her meal tickets. After she ate, she got a good rubdown on her very pregnant belly and crashed on the chaise lounge outside.

The next morning she came in for breakfast—very light on her feet and not pregnant. I knew she had had the kittens in the courtyard and sure enough, there were five beautiful kittens in the bushes by our guest house. We could not help but sneak peeks at them, although we really did try to stay away and let her have her mommy time with them. While we were excited to again witness the wonderful experience of Ali being a mama, we remained committed to this being her last time.

Ali-Mama and her offspring spent all their days in the "birth bushes" until the day I caught her out of the corner of my eye with kitten in mouth. She jumped up onto the platform of our decorative urn, which is about six feet high. She then proceeded to jump up onto the rim of the urn, which was another three feet high. Finally, she jumped down into it. In my mind's eye, I can still see her tail as she descended into the bowl of this huge, deep urn. She then did the same with the other four kittens. It was fortuitous that I happened to see her do it because late that afternoon we were hit by a torrential downpour. The rain was filling the urn quickly and it would only have been a matter of minutes before the feline family would surely have met their demise.

My husband and I went into emergency rescue mode. He got an umbrella and a ladder and proceeded to climb up next to the urn. I was standing at the base of the urn with a basket in which to place the kittens. When Ali saw Allan with the umbrella she startled and jumped out of the urn and over the wall. Even in this tenuous situation, while Allan handed me the kittens one by one, I could not help but to "ooh" and "ahh" over each one. Had I not seen Ali go into the urn, our little feline family would surely have drowned.

We placed the kittens in the office closet with the famous beach towel from the previous nest. We opened the sliding door hoping Ali would come back quickly to tend to the mewing babies. Again, she did not disappoint. She came back soaking wet and ready to nurse, always the great mom during those first few months. There were four yellow tabbies and one beige tabby, all with those glorious green eyes.

By this time Allan and I were old hands at being kitty grandparents and we loved every minute of it. Before long they were scampering around the house and causing havoc, which we thoroughly enjoyed.

I was curious about the kittens being yellow tabbies, since they were different from the others Ali had spawned. One evening my questions were aptly answered. We came home to find not six felines on the patio but seven. I did a double take. There was one cat too many. Ali had never been friendly to any other cat in the neighborhood and would chase any intruder viciously away. Yet there in the twilight was a very large—you guessed it—yellow tabby male. Clearly it was their dad.

It was such an unbelievable sight to behold. The big yellow guy and Ali lounging in the courtyard with all five kittens playfully hopping over both of them—one big happy family. My daughter who was visiting us at the time named him Garfield. Garfield was unquestionably feral and would not let me near him. In spite of that you could tell he was a gentle soul and that Ali approved of him, so he was fine in my book. We welcomed him into the Markoff family and he soon discovered getting three squares and a chaise lounge made our courtyard a darn good place to be. He would come and go often and whenever he came back, Ali and kittens always welcomed him with open paws.

One day he arrived on the patio, in terrible shape, barely able to walk. He clearly had been in a fight. At first, I thought he had lost his eye. Upon closer inspection, which was not so easy because I still could not get close to him, I realized it was still intact but I could see he was very badly injured. He really needed medical attention, but there was no way I would have been able to capture him. I called my vet, and he prescribed an antibiotic which I mixed with milk. Garfield lapped it up. Unfortunately, it was not enough. He stayed around for a couple of days then left, never to be seen again. I had heard that when animals know it is their time to leave this world they go off by themselves to die. I believe that is what happened to our big guy, Garfield.

ALI-MAMA

The time was fast approaching when we needed to make a decision about Ali and the kittens. I knew that Ali had to finally be spayed and the kittens either spayed or neutered and adopted. We also needed to get Ali out of our community, which was on a mission to trap and euthanize all resident ferals. There were many meetings where ridiculous reasons were given for this new initiative. When one woman was asked why she wanted the cats gone she said it was because they walk across the corner of her lawn in the middle of the night. I have learned through experience that when people do not like animals they tend to be irrational—my opinion—just saying. I knew it was just a matter of time before Ali would be captured. I was not about to let that happen.

A perfect solution appeared—my daughter, Michelle. During my daughter's many trips to

A FERAL CAT'S TALE

Florida, she built a very close, loving relationship with Ali who clearly returned those sentiments. Michelle had been thinking about adopting a cat and I thought this was a perfect solution. However, we needed to convince Ali to become a New York City apartment cat. I do not know if it was a leap of faith or just plain crazy to think that Ali could adjust to apartment living. I knew she was getting worn out from having three litters a year and I thought maybe it was time for her to retire with someone who loved her as much as we did. Since the last litter of kittens, Ali became quite docile and loved attention. She did not have the need to prowl as much as she once did, so spent a great deal of time in the house. Ali had developed a confidence in us and I knew she would do the same with Michelle. I was so hoping that this solution would be good for Ali. I already knew it would be great for Michelle.

ALI-MAMA

In February 2004 Michelle flew down to Florida and we began making plans for Ali's trip to New York. We were able to put her and the kittens into the crate for our trip to the veterinarian. The kittens got a clean bill of health and believe it or not, no worms. The vet could never understand why neither Ali nor any of her progeny were infested with worms. When I told him that Ali would never drink regular water she would only drink pool water, we surmised that the chemicals in the pool water rid her and her kittens of parasites.

Ali was surprisingly calm during all this hoopla and accepted with ease all that was happening to her. I think she knew whatever we were doing was because we loved her so. She got a clean bill of health, a health certificate and now Ali-Mama was ready for the Big Apple. Don't think I did not say to myself that this was the

A FERAL CAT'S TALE

A FERAL CAT'S TALE

craziest idea—a feral cat adapting to life in a New York City apartment—but we forged ahead. Ali-Mama was about to take the final leg of her Feral Cat's Tale with Michelle right by her side.

Ali-Mama must have known this was her destiny because she cooperated through every phase of this journey. She let us place her in the flight bag, she was acceptably good on the plane and together my daughter and Ali landed uneventfully in New York City, ready for their new life together.

I can only relay the remainder of the story through the eyes of my daughter, who like us also grew to love this wonderful not-so-feral cat. There were a few blips like the fact the Ali-Mama did not use the litter box for about five days. We checked with Peanut and Blue's vet, who assured us that it was not unusual during this period of adjustment. Ali also spent a great deal of time under the bed but as each day passed she became a little more confident and started exploring her surroundings. When she finally used the litter box we almost took an ad out in *The New York Times* to express our excitement and relief.

I can only imagine what she must have thought when she became brave enough to sit on the window sill and look out the 25th floor of a New York City highrise. What, no salamanders or birds? Nothing green? She did not seem to mind and formed a wonderful attachment to Michelle.

Ali became very comfortable and confident in her new life. In March of 2004 Michelle tore her ACL skiing. She had to have surgery and came home with a humongous apparatus to exercise her leg. Ali reverted back to her old skittish self and at first she wanted no part of this torture device. But she must have sensed that Michelle was needy and in pain because even though she was afraid she braved this device to comfort Michelle and stay by her side. Once you have earned a cat's loyalty and love they will demonstrate that time and time again.

The feral-human relationship grew warmly as I had suspected it would. In July 2004 Michelle was offered a new position in Basking Ridge, New Jersey which required that she and Ali relocate. Ali made the move with Michelle and settled into her new town house with ease. We could not believe how this feral cat seemed to always rise to the occasion. She was able to sit on the window sill and actually see birds and green trees. I am sure she loved the upgrade.

Ali, always in keeping with her catitude, insisted on very specific sleeping arrangements. Michelle had to sleep on her stomach so Ali could curl up in the small of Michelle's back after they were tucked in for the night. If Michelle happened to be on her back, Ali would sit upright and stare at Michelle until Position A was assumed. It was as if Ali was saying to Michelle— get with the program, you know I like to sleep on your back. It goes without saying that Michelle always complied.

While Ali was giving Michelle emotional support, Michelle was providing much enjoyed massage therapy sessions. During one of the sessions Michelle found a pea size growth on the left side of Ali's breast bone. Michelle, who was an administrator for Memorial Sloan-Kettering Cancer Center, tried not to panic and think the worst upon this discovery. She kept her always positive approach and made an appointment with a feline veterinarian.

The vet took a biopsy and the waiting began. The diagnosis was indeed a cancerous mass on her mammary gland. I learned this is a common condition in cats who have had many litters, which is yet another reason in support of spaying felines. The vet was not optimistic but felt that Ali should be taken to a specialist who would remove the mass, then start radiation and chemotherapy.

Michelle was well aware that there were many paths to take when faced with what is often a fatal prognosis. She was conflicted as to whether it would be humane to subject Ali, first to the surgery, then to the subsequent torturous treatments. We were always cognizant of the fact that Ali was born feral and always tried to treat her in a way that respected her feral-ness. Michelle decided to make an appointment with our family veterinarian, Dr. Phillip Stewart. I have known Dr. Stewart for many years and have the utmost respect for his ability to bring clarity, humaneness and common sense to heart wrenching situations. I have known him to strongly guard against anthropomorphizing, which means attributing human values and feelings to animals. He explained that when you make decisions for animals based upon human values, those decisions are not always what is in the best interest of the animal. I think that most people who truly love their pets have a strong tendency to do just that. Michelle and I were no different.

In September Michelle drove to Middletown, New York for Ali-Mama's appointment with Dr. Stewart. He examined her, took an x-ray and confirmed that although the tumor was small there was also lung involvement. Since the tumor was not causing her discomfort his advice was to do nothing. Dr. Stewart explained to Michelle that he felt subjecting animals to pain and suffering which they did not understand, even when the prognosis was dire, was inhumane. This conflict between euthanasia and administering extraordinary treatment exists not only in the animal kingdom but in the human species as well. Do humans have the right to choose their destiny and the destiny of their pets? There is no right answer but of this I am sure—the answer lies in one's heart.

Dr. Stewart said he had no way of knowing how long Ali would live but he strongly believed that Ali's fate should be left in hands that are bigger than ours. He said take her home and love her. He also told Michelle that she would know when it was time for Ali-Mama to cross onto the rainbow bridge.

The time following the diagnosis was sad but Michelle and Ali continued to bond. Michelle tried to put it out of her mind but she knew that Ali was on borrowed time. Michelle treated every day with Ali as a most precious gift and did just what Dr. Stewart told her to do—love her.

Ali was asymptomatic for a little over a year until January of 2006, when she started bleeding from the tumor. Michelle brought her back to Dr. Stewart, who felt that since she was fairly healthy and had been enjoying a good quality of life, he could remove it with little discomfort.

After the operation Michelle took her home and moved the litter box from upstairs to the main floor so Ali would not have to climb stairs. Ali's catitude again reared its head in the months following the tumor removal. The moment there was anything in the litter box Ali expected Michelle to clean it, pronto. She would sit upright and stare at the box then look at Michelle and continue to do so until Michelle finally understood it was her mission in life to keep that litter box completely poop and pee free. Talk about non-verbal communication!

Ali had a loving, happy couple of months after the surgery before she stopped eating and losing weight. Those of us who have had to make the decision to euthanize a beloved pet know the decision does not come easily. It is an agonizing process but, again, Dr. Stewart was right when he said Michelle would know when it was time.

Michelle made that dreaded call to me and we spoke about the decision that was before us. We both knew in our heart of hearts that it was the right one for Ali. I felt strongly that I wanted some time with Ali, so I drove to New Jersey to pick up Michelle and Ali-Mama and bring them to Dr. Stewart. I made sure Michelle was able to spend one on one time with Ali on the drive back to New York. We went on that final journey together—Mom, Michelle and Ali-Mama.

ALI-MAMA

Dr. Stewart and his staff ("of the two Karens" as we called them) were so kind and compassionate. We were sending her to the great beyond with all of the warmth and love she had shown us over the years. When Dr. Stewart closed her eyes, I imagined we were sending her to kitty heaven where there would be plenty of salamanders, gefilte fish, and Fancy Feast—but no fleas. She would be able to fly over the pearly gates as she had our courtyard wall and have the best time with Garfield who I knew was waiting for her. Seeing all of her beautiful babies—maybe not so much!

Michelle and I shed many tears together and then made arrangements to have Ali's ashes shipped to Florida. We felt it was fitting that she should travel full circle and rest where she lived free as a feral. We flew to Florida the next day to await her arrival.

A FERAL CAT'S TALE

Ali-Mama and Nancy together for the last time

When we received the package Allan, Michelle and I went out to the courtyard bushes to lovingly spread her ashes. It was then that I realized with sadness that this was the end of Ali-Mama: A Feral Cat's Tale.

ALI-MAMA

MICHELLE'S EPILOGUE

Ali-Mama taught me about life...how to protect, survive, adapt, cede control, tolerate, accept, grieve and love. She made the old adage of "it's better to have loved and lost than never to have loved at all" mean something to me. Six years later, I still cry sometimes when thinking of her because I'm sad that she is gone but I would never give up the cherished memories I have of her or the adventures we shared. As more time passes, however, my sadness is replaced by gratitude that I had the privilege to care for this wonderful, precious soul in her golden years where all she had to worry about was a clean litter box.

EPILOGUE

Some would say that I saved Ali-Mama's life. I say she taught me lessons that helped me live mine.

As I look back at all those joyous and laughable moments, I realize the simplicity of a feral cat's life. They create joy in their own world, find mates, bear kittens, teach those kittens how to survive in their world and determine their own destiny. And if along the way they find a special human with whom to create a bond not only do they enrich their life, the life of that human is enriched beyond measure. Mine certainly was.

This glorious creature always pulled at my heart strings and continued to do so until the day she died.

ALI-MAMA

Michelle will never get over Ali-Mama but she has found a new furry feline to fill her heart and home. In the heat of August 2007, a beautiful gray and white cat showed up at our office in New York. True to his nature, my husband started feeding him and before we knew it they were fast friends. I think the Markoffs subliminally give off messages to any creature that happens to need food, shelter and a little love.

We tried to find the cat's owner to no avail. He had a collar but no other identification. We took him to Dr. Stewart who examined him, gave him a clean bill of health and confirmed he was not micro-chipped. He also gave us a cream to apply to his paws which were badly burned from walking on the hot summer pavement. I called Michelle to tell her the good news, and that I now had to now find him a loving home. In a moment this beautiful big boy, sight unseen, had a new home with Michelle. I drove him to New Jersey and when I arrived it was love at first sight for the two of them. She named this handsome guy Tai. They have since moved from New Jersey to Colorado and then to Connecticut where Michelle is an administrator for the Yale Cancer Center at Smilow Cancer Hospital. They continue to live happily ever after.

Allan's and my love of animals continues to grow and if we had the space we would certainly be a safe house to any animal in need. Allan and I take great joy in Peanut and Blue who are now twelve years old. Every time I look at Peanut, who is a mirrored carbon copy of her mom, I remember Ali-Mama and all the joy we had and lessons learned. When I am at our home in Florida the memory and love of Ali-Mama is always present she will never be forgotten. We have since added a red toy poodle named Sassicaia and a white toy poodle named Enzo to our family. They are all the joys of our lives.

As I was doing the final editing on this tale in my Florida home, my husband called me to come look out at the courtyard. Sitting there looking in the same door Ali-Mama and her kittens went in and out of so often was an exact replica of Ali-Mama's daughter Peanut. My heart skipped and wonderful memories came flooding back. Then I said to myself—oh no, not again! I went to the cabinet and brought out the Fancy Feast.

When I opened the door, as I expected she ran, but not too far. I placed the dish of food on the patio and she guardedly started to gobble it up. She was indeed a hungry kitty. When filling the dish for the second time I got close enough to see her beautiful face and those gorgeous green eyes. She surely is a descendent of the soon to be famous Ali-Mama. I also saw her left ear had been

A FERAL CAT'S TALE

eartipped. Trap, neuter and return is the only program that will free these ferals from unnecessary euthanization. Here was proof positive that the Humane Society of the United State's program of TNR was working in my community.

The plight of the feral cat has reached epic proportions and the need for education and implementation of the trap, neuter, return programs have never been more essential.

If Ali-Mama has left her mark on you, as she has on all whose lives she touched, please honor her memory by getting involved with your local humane society to assist in controlling this terrible overpopulation problem and maybe one day end the suffering of these glorious creatures.

Website: http://www.alimamaaferalcatstale.com/
Facebook: Ali-Mama: A Feral Cat's Tale
Twitter: @Alimamaferalcat